WHAT'S BENEATH

PEEKING UNDER the HOOD

by Esther Porter   illustrated by Andrés Lozano

PICTURE WINDOW BOOKS
a capstone imprint

Cars are cool!

See the **shiny** wheels? Hear the engine **growl?**

Hear the **honking** horn?
Feel the wind **blowing**
through the open windows?

You've seen cars from the outside. They come in many sizes, shapes,
and colors. But what do cars look like beneath the hood?
Turn the page for a peek ...

A car has many parts. Some parts work together to start the car and make it move. Some parts stop it. Others keep the car and its passengers cool. Parts that work together make up a system. Auto technicians check car systems. They use computers to find problems.

If something is wrong, auto technicians try to fix it. They may need to install new parts.

Power Up!

An engine gives a car power. Thousands of small explosions happen inside an engine every minute. The explosions move the car forward. Each explosion happens inside a cylinder. Most cars have four to eight cylinders. The cylinders work together. They move pistons up and down. Pistons act like your legs pedaling a bike.

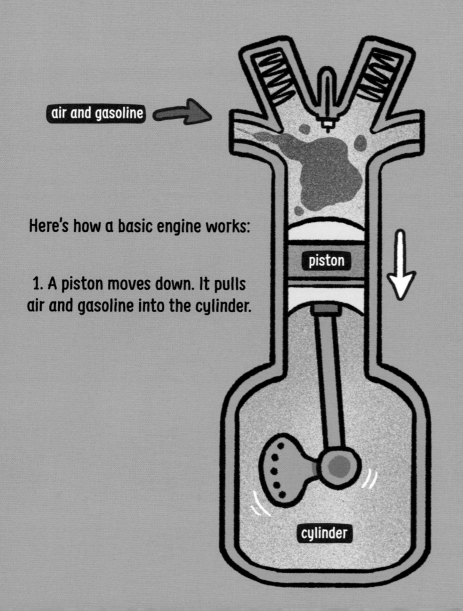

air and gasoline

piston

cylinder

Here's how a basic engine works:

1. A piston moves down. It pulls air and gasoline into the cylinder.

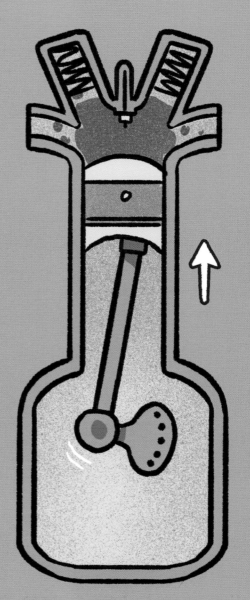

2. The piston moves up. It squeezes the air and gasoline.

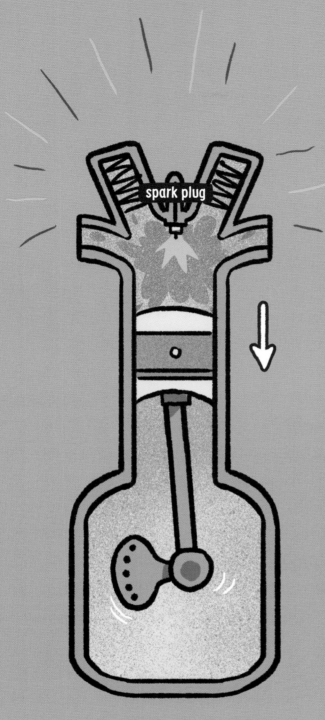

spark plug

3. A spark plug ignites the
squeezed air and gasoline.
BOOM!
The explosion pushes the
piston back down again.

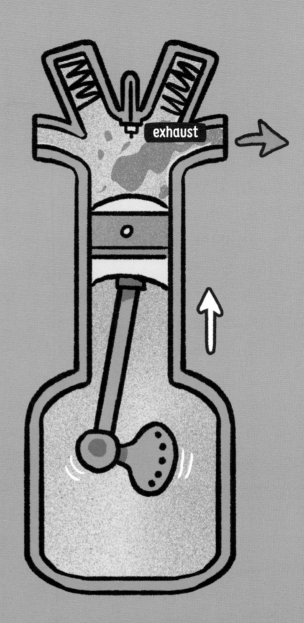

exhaust

4. The piston moves back up.
It pushes the exhaust from
the cylinder.

Add the Gas

What powers the engine? **Fuel!** Next time you visit a gas station, watch your parents. See how they add gasoline to the car's fuel tank. When a car is running, a fuel pump sends gas from the tank to the engine. Press the gas pedal, and air is sent to the engine too.

Exhaust is a mixture of used-up gas and air. See how it leaves a car? It goes through the muffler and out the tailpipe.

Keep Cool

It gets hot under the hood! A car engine needs to keep cool. If it overheats it won't work. Oil helps keep an engine from getting too hot. Coolant also helps. It flows through a hose and small holes around the engine. The coolant pulls away heat.

Time to Move

How does the power in an engine move a car forward? The transmission. Remember how the pistons move up and down like pedals on a bike? Your bike needs to switch gears for more power. So does a car. The pistons need a set of gears to send more power to the wheels.

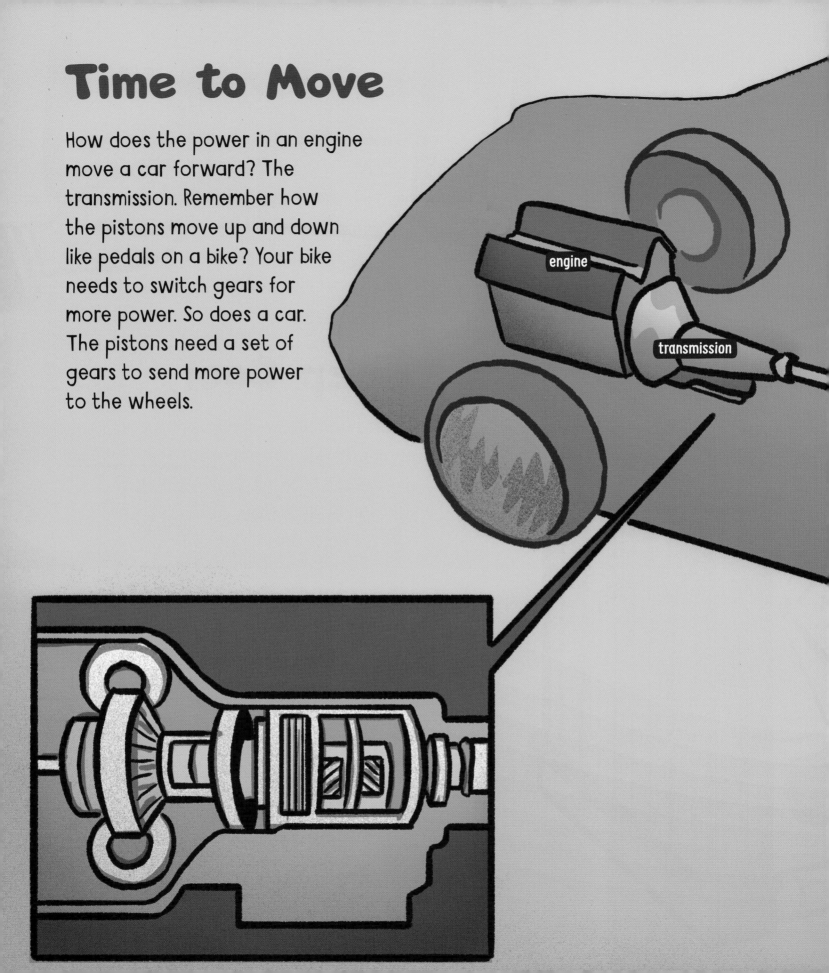

engine

transmission

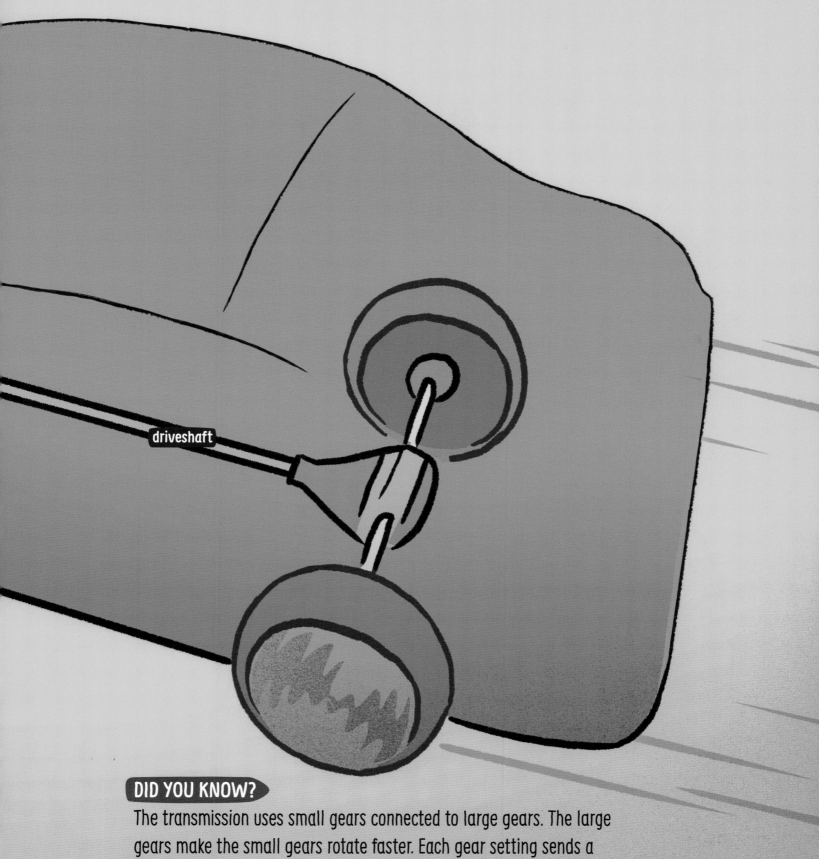

driveshaft

The transmission uses small gears connected to large gears. The large gears make the small gears rotate faster. Each gear setting sends a different amount of power to the wheels. To reach the back wheels, power is sent through a driveshaft.

Flowing Here, Flowing There

Just like your body, a car needs lots of fluids. An engine needs oil to run smoothly and keep from overheating. The transmission needs fluid too. Fluid allows the gears to switch and keeps the gears in position. Cars also need brake fluid and power steering fluid.

brake fluid

DID YOU KNOW?

Unlike air, liquid does not compress (get smaller). So we use liquid to lock things into place. Transmission fluid locks gears. Braking fluid stops the wheels. Power steering fluid allows the steering wheel and tires to turn.

Just a Spark

What is the first thing your parents do to start the car? They turn the key in the ignition. Turning the key pulls power from the battery to start the car. The battery holds a car's electrical power. Once the car wakes up, the alternator takes over. The alternator is near the front of the engine.

battery

alternator

The alternator powers the headlights, brake lights, and turn signals. It powers the dashboard displays. It recharges the battery and runs the car's computer.

ignition switch

Does a car have a brain?
Yes! Sort of.

A computer acts like a car's brain. It makes sure the engine is getting enough power. It sets the transmission to the right gear. It makes sure the brakes are working. It control's the air temperature inside the car. The computer also triggers warning lights when something is wrong.

Hot and Cold

Cars don't do well if they are too hot or too cold. Neither do their passengers! There are systems to keep people comfortable. If it's cold outside, a heater warms people. A fan blows air across the heater and into the car. **Toasty!**

When it's hot outside, an air conditioner cools people.

A Car Skeleton

What holds a car together? The chassis (rhymes with "classy"). The chassis is like a car skeleton. All of a car's parts are attached to it.

The chassis gives a car its shape. The chassis holds a car's engine and suspension. The suspension absorbs the bumps in the road. It also keeps the car from bouncing, so you don't get carsick.

Stop!

Now you know what makes a car go. How does it stop? Think about the bike again. When you press the brake lever, pads press against the tire. The tire stops.

master cylinder (pistons)

brake pedal

Pressing the brake pedal in a car works much the same way. Brake fluid presses into pistons. The pistons make the brake pads squeeze the brake rotors. The rotors help slow and then stop the car's turning wheels.

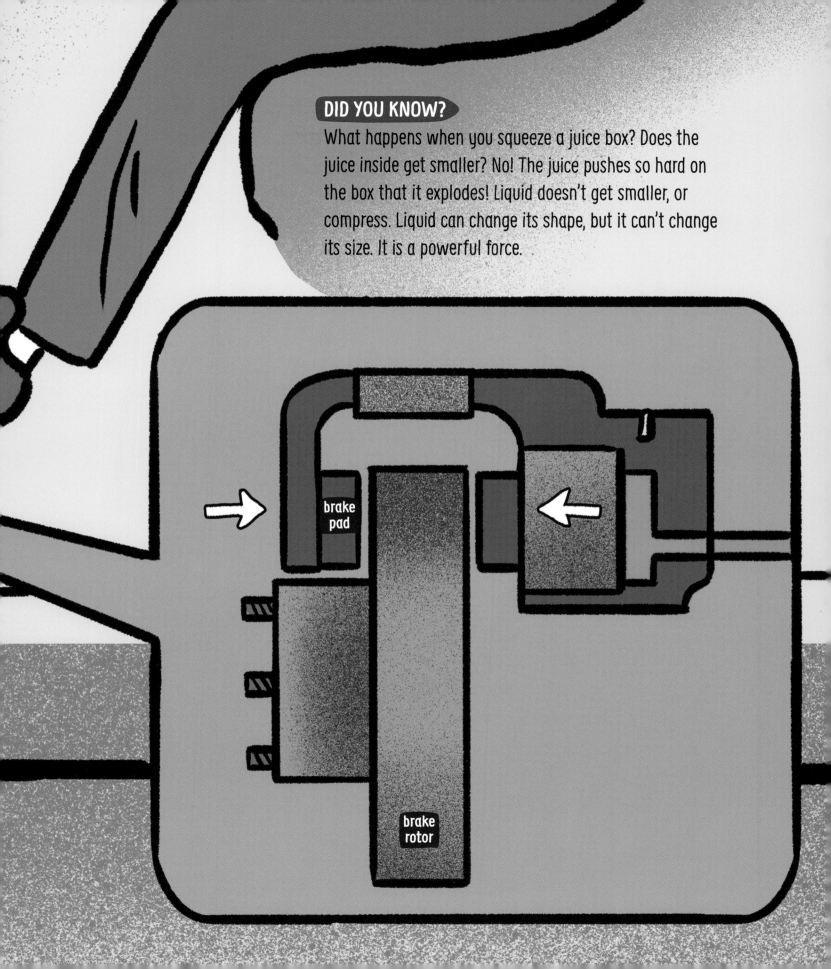

DID YOU KNOW?

What happens when you squeeze a juice box? Does the juice inside get smaller? No! The juice pushes so hard on the box that it explodes! Liquid doesn't get smaller, or compress. Liquid can change its shape, but it can't change its size. It is a powerful force.

brake pad

brake rotor

Rolling Along

Tires are the only parts of a car that touch the road. They're made of tough rubber. Tires have grooves to help them grip the road. The grooves are called tread. Air-filled tires help a car roll smoothly. When a car rolls smoothly, it uses less gas. Why? A rough ride makes an engine work hard. The engine needs more power to move the car. More power means more gas.

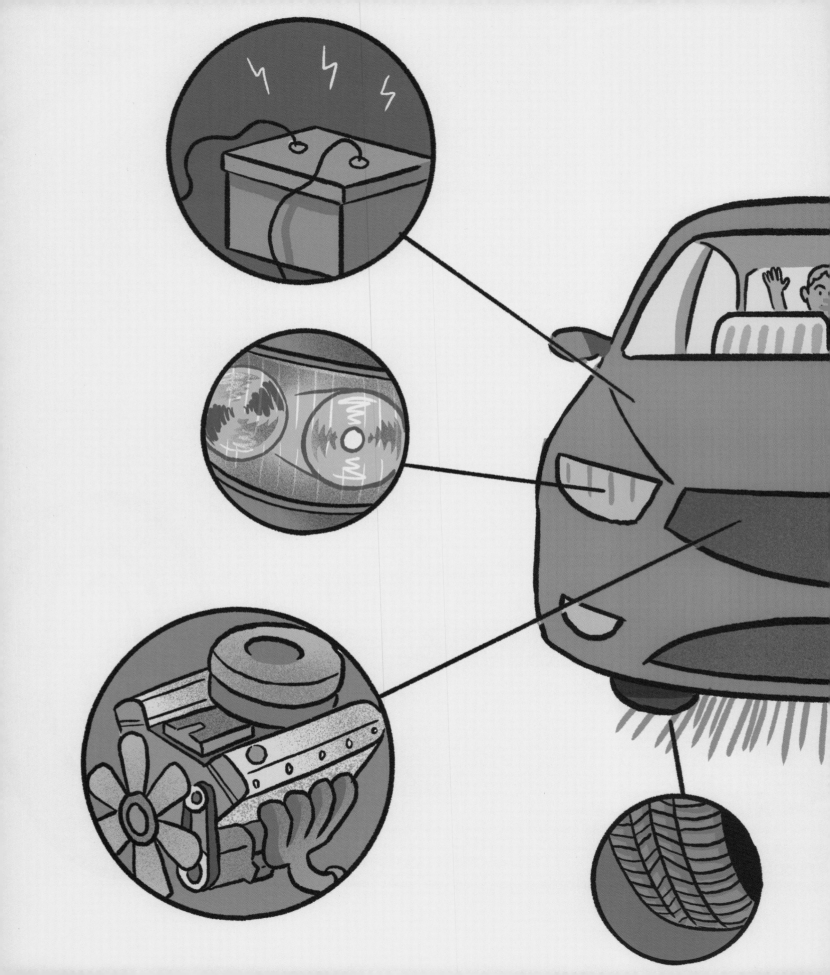

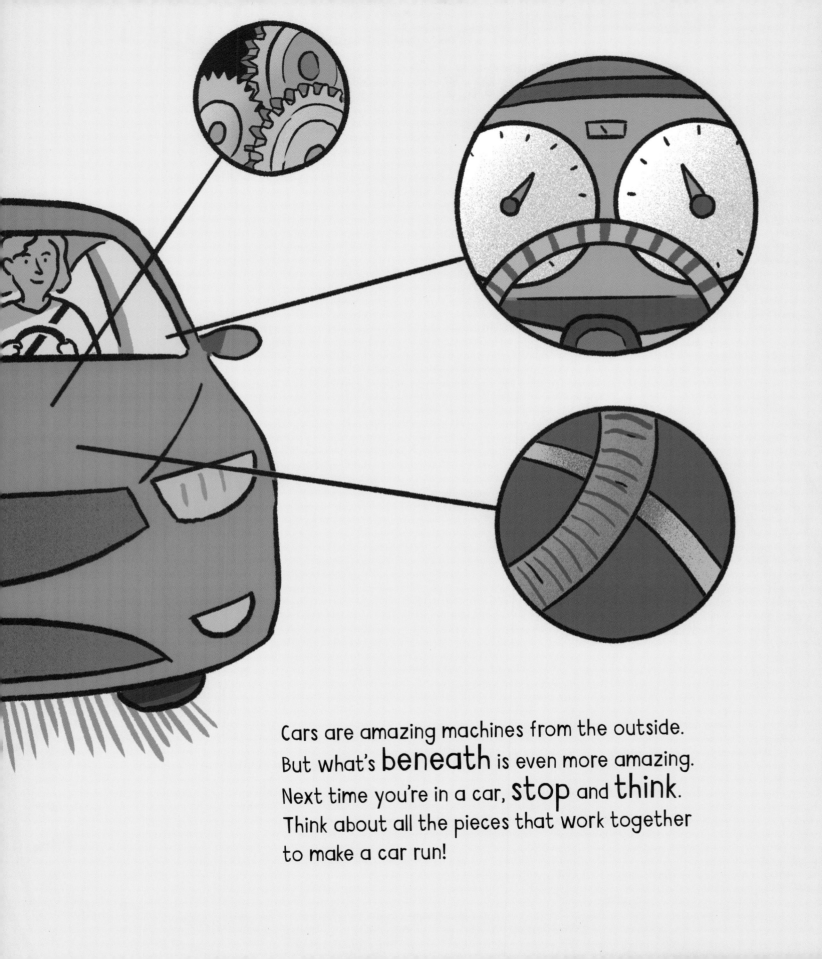

Cars are amazing machines from the outside. But what's **beneath** is even more amazing. Next time you're in a car, **stop** and **think**. Think about all the pieces that work together to make a car run!

GLOSSARY

absorb—to soak up

auto technician—a person who fixes vehicles or machinery; also called an auto tech

chassis—the frame or skeleton of a car

coolant—a mixture of water and antifreeze that flows through an engine and carries off heat

cylinder—a metal chamber; standard cars have four to eight cylinders in an engine

driveshaft—the part of a vehicle that carries power from the transmission gears to the wheels

engine—a machine that makes the power needed to move something

exhaust—a mixture of used-up gas and air that comes out of a car's tailpipe

gear—a toothed wheel that fits into another toothed wheel

ignite—to cause something to burn

install—to put in

piston—part of an engine that moves up and down within a cylinder

rotate—to spin around

spark plug—a device that ignites the air and gas inside an engine

suspension—the system of springs and shock absorbers that absorbs a car's up-and-down movements

transmission—the series of gears that sends power from the engine to the wheels

CRITICAL THINKING USING THE COMMON CORE

1. Look back at the images on pages 24 and 25. Describe how the braking system stops a car. (Key Ideas and Details)

2. The suspension is what keeps a car from bouncing over bumps in the road. What do you think it would be like to drive over a gravel road without a suspension? (Integration of Knowledge and Ideas)

3. What do auto technicians do? Why are they important? (Integration of Knowledge and Ideas)

READ MORE

Eason, Sarah. *How Does a Car Work?* How Does It Work? New York: Gareth Stevens Pub., 2010.

Harris, Nicholas. *Car.* How It Works. Hauppauge, N.Y.: Barron's Educational Series, 2010.

Parker, Steve. *Cars, Trucks, and Bikes.* How It Works. Broomall, Penn.: Mason Crest Publishers, 2011.

INTERNET SITES

FactHound offers a safe, fun way to find Internet sites related to this book. All of the sites on FactHound have been researched by our staff.

Here's all you do:

Visit www.facthound.com

Type in this code: 9781479586677

 **Super-cool stuff!** Check out projects, games and lots more at www.capstonekids.com

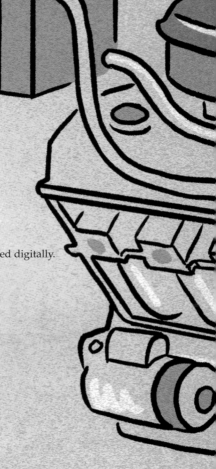

Special thanks to our adviser, Sheldon Newkirk, Automotive Instructor, Blackhawk Technical College, for his expertise.

Picture Window Books are published by Capstone, 1710 Roe Crest Drive, North Mankato, Minnesota 56003 www.mycapstone.com

Editor: Jill Kalz
Designer: Russell Griesmer
Creative Director: Nathan Gassman
Production Specialist: Katy LaVigne
The illustrations in this book were created digitally.

Printed and bound in US
007536CGS16

Library of Congress Cataloging-in-Publication Data
Cataloging-in-publication information is on file with the Library of Congress.
ISBN 978-1-4795-8667-7 (library binding)
ISBN 978-1-4795-8671-4 (paperback)
ISBN 978-1-4795-8675-2 (eBook PDF)

LOOK FOR ALL THE BOOKS IN THE SERIES: